You are an

Amazing Teacher

because

To my **Teacher**

From: _____

Date: _____

The best thing about you
is your

_____

Thank you for being
patient with me when

_____

You are more awesome than

_____

You should win the grand
prize for

_____

You have an amazing talent for

_____

You are always
encouraging me to

_____

It's really helpful when you

_____

You make learning fun by

_____

You taught me how to

_____

You deserve a year's
supply of

_____

I wish all teachers could

_____

as well as you do

It really helps me when you

_____

You should be in charge
of

_____

You have given me the
confidence to

_____

You make me laugh when you

_____

You make learning

_____

easy!

You were there for me

_____

You have
inspired me to

_____

Because of you
I can

_____

The best thing you taught me was

_____

I will remember you
telling me to

_____

You are an amazing
teacher because

_____